GRIMOIRE

GRIMOIRE

CHERENE SHERRARD

AUTUMN
HOUSE PRESS

Autumn House Press receives state arts funding support through a grant from the Pennsylvania Council on the Arts, a state agency funded by the Commonwealth of Pennsylvania, and the National Endowment for the Arts, a federal agency.

Cover art: Joscelyn Gardner, *Convolvulus jalapa (Yara)*, 2010, hand-coloured stone lithograph on frosted mylar, 36" x 24", copyright the artist (www.joscelyngardner.org). Photo credit: John Tamblyn.
Cover design: Melissa Dias-Mandoly

ISBN: 978-1-938769-60-3
LCCN: 2020936527

A Note on the Text

Certain italicized sections of *Grimoire* are transcribed and/or adapted from one of the earliest cookbooks published by an African American woman: Mrs. Malinda Russell's *A Domestic Cook Book: Containing a Careful Selection of Useful Receipts for the Kitchen* (1866). A "receipt" is an early spelling of recipe; it is also used for formula, remedy, or cure.

For the mothers

Table of Contents

I.

II.

GRIMOIRE

I.

Miranda, Malinda

I am not the wizard's daughter.
My father never taught me how
to bewitch a sprite, ensnare
an Indian, or summon storms.
Still, I mistake the receipt book
for a hedge witch's apothecary:
A Domestic Cook Book by
Malinda Russell, A Woman of Color,
Paw Paw, Michigan, 1866. I am as
struck by the similarity of our names
as by the curiosity of our circumstances.
The correct pronunciation is Mi-*rin*-da,
not Mir-ran-da. Like Malinda, I have a son
in need of special consideration. We are
far from home. Sales of this book
of sustenance sustain a free woman
plying a trade at the finale of the Civil War.
Well matched are our aims.

To My Followers

The economy of the receipts requires much creativity on my part.
Full disclosure: I am an amateur. Trust I will scrupulously test
any modification before posting to ensure consistent, if not
excellent, results. Where I have substituted, I will make a note
as well as provide the original receipt at the start of each entry.
If your achievements exceed mine, share in the comments,
along with any questions or concerns.

Marble Cake

The White:

My son, ½ cup white flour, ¼ cup brown sugar,
has trouble with fractions. When pregnant
I did not follow instructions, *beat the yolks and sugar*
together until very light. It was months before I accepted
I was carrying another human being, add ½ pound butter,
whip fourteen egg whites, *flavor with lemon, half gill brandy.*

The Dark:

The ophthalmologist suspects that he's color-blind,
½ cup molasses, the yolks of eight eggs. Perhaps
that is why he prefers brown sugar in his oatmeal.
He can't tell how it's different from white, *flavor with*
cinnamon, cloves, nutmeg, or mace. I confess,
I palmed the iron pills, drank light roast brews
without sugar or cream. Mixed children usually
come out beautifully. The doctor is unsure about mine.
Paper and butter the pan, first a layer of the white,
then of the dark, alternately finishing with the white.

Wild Yeast

What color is Shakespeare?
To answer, I read my son Dunbar.
First, we recite "We Wear the Mask,"
then "When Malindy Sings."
We pause at the line
f'om de kitchen to de big woods.
When cooking with Malinda,
her haintly breath is citrus and clove.
Her hands, rough as wind within,
smooth as pears without, guide me
as I knead and read her receipts aloud.
Each line works its alchemy,
solidifies her shade, elevates
the timbre of her voice.
She does not speak the broken tongue
of Paul's folksy muse.
Penwomanship alone affirms
her education. Not until
the poet delivers Dinah's arms,
buried elbow-deep in dough,
do I forgive his lyric blasphemy.

Restoring the Hair to Its Original Color

They don't tell you how it will age you:
the lack of sleep, the cracked nipples,
the constant buzzing, and running
hither and thither. When he was born,
my son's hair was black and slick.
As he grew, it curled, then bronzed
like his father's. What started as
a silver streak over my left temple
spread like a platinum coronet.
I dare you to combine *two drachms*
of Lac Sulphuris with eight ounces
of rose water. Shake thoroughly,
apply every night before bed.

Crossed Stars

For our English unit, I decide on Shakespeare.
We'll read then write an English sonnet. We'll go
See *Romeo and Juliet* at the American Players,
Taking advantage of the homeschool special.
A row of single mothers and our single charges.
The children will sit together, the mothers behind,
Or, the children will sit alternately, a mother between,
Or, we will sit two and two: in pairs, parent and partner.
A matinee sun directly overhead. Discounted
Seats throw no shade. We melt the amphitheater.
Neither hats nor parasols allowed, so mothers fan
Whichever child is on whatever side, and we
Can barely recall whatsoever if it was the moon
Or the nurse or the poison that betrayed the lovers.

Things to Do with Ginger

Three kinds of ginger blent in the bowl
I stir while wearing a white evening gown,
standard wardrobe issue for Ginger Grant.
All one needs on a desert island. Of all
the castaways, she is the one whose body,
stretched into sequins of spun sugar,
I long to occupy. The way she exhales
each syllable is the exact balance
of heat and sweet that must align
for gingerbread to be edible and not
something survivors of the S.S. Minnow
wouldn't touch. The oven fans the air
effervescent with copper dust.
I can't take my eyes off the caramel.
Not even to tie an apron over my ivory
taffeta, which is, in fact, my unworn
wedding dress, now tight across the bodice
but still so loose in the tail of tulle that my
son is lost in its folds. In my episode,
Ginger marries the Professor
after pushing that insipid Mary Ann
out to sea on a bamboo raft. I imagine
sharks tearing at her manicured toes,
drawn to the crimson polish that must
have been her one personal item.
Sponge cake soaked in coconut rum,
spangled with shards of crystallized ginger,
is perfect for tropical nuptials. Our
fortunate couple can easily keep their
vows in a space where the other
single woman has been set adrift.

A Tempest in a Teapot

Officers have come to my home
to inquire about my son's truancy.
The resource page for the network
of homeschoolers has not prepared
me to manage the legal loopholes
of a surprise visit. I offer them slices
of Malinda's Strawberry Short Cake.

Split the cake while hot, butter well
and cover with berries, stake in a steak dish,
turn sweet cream over it, and eat while hot for tea.

I explain that I have a curriculum and a degree
—mortgages were once my forte, an irony
given our house is currently underwater.
I lie about my marital status. Widows,
I have learned, are more sympathetic,
even if they keep their maiden names.
My son makes his timid appearance.
He is small for his age, a charmer with
blue-framed glasses and cowlicked hair.
What a beautiful boy, says the female officer.
They leave hurriedly, lips stained berry-red.

IEP (Individualized Education Plan)

As part of the agreement with the school board, I have succumbed,
or rather my son has submitted, to an assessment.

The school psychologist puts her hand on his head.
I see her fingers wrap around his curls as if pulling a comb
through porcupine quills. My hand twitches. If I slap her
before she completes the examination, it may bias the diagnosis.

Malinda's Last Day at the Patisserie

Union soldiers spotted in Macon's woods
The town arming its leftover menfolk
Past time to box the glass pedestals
Return borrowed linens to ladies
Whose kitchens I toiled in
Sacks of flour to the church
How quiet the street
As if it were already Sunday
War makes folly of time
I catch a whiff of magnolia
See Susan Harris's tree aflame
We arrive in Paw Paw, sifted
snow still on the ground

Fair Trade

Before Malinda became a chef,
she was a laundress. I wish she
had included with her receipts
a secret for getting beet juice
out of an apron before adding
pickled beets to her repertoire.
My Formica has taken on
a magenta hue. Although
I scrub with old remedies—
baking soda, peroxide—
days later it still blushes.

Sycorax's Lament

After leaving her son such a legacy,
it's shocking how easily he's deprived
of it by a shipwrecked trickster.
My son wants to know why fruitcake
has so little fruit in it. Malinda calls for
one gill rose water, one wine-glass brandy,
currants, raisins, and citron, which is like
a lemon in the same way that a cherry is
like a raspberry. They are both reddish
and small, but the similarity ends there.
I imagine her sass had a zesty flavor
but not enough to give offense. Cheek,
I have found, doesn't serve us well.
You can substitute a key lime and have
satisfactory results, but what is a key lime
when you have had an orchard.

Grimoire

Mirror, mirror:
show me that world
where black, gay, male,
dyslexic are
adjectives
of excellence,
achievement, not
devastation.

Cut-Woman

We give the American pastime a go.
Dominican? The coach raises a hopeful
eyebrow at my son's Spanish last name.
I shrug, maybe it will give us an edge
with the World Series of fathers drawing
straws to coach my son's little league team.

Before baseball was boxing:
a large purple elephant hung
from the ceiling fan in his bedroom
and served as a punching bag.
I wound two-ply toilet paper around
his fists, sat on a stool in the corner,
and waited for him to unravel.

The Challenger is a coed league
for kids disabled by life's whimsy.
Seated in the bleachers in fall,
leaves drifting on the yellowing
field, I can't put the grainy image of
the Challenger out of my head,
on a split screen I imagine a different
set of parents, sunburned, who
don't cheer for the opposing team,
every walk, run, or foul, but instead
bellow at the umpire, high-fiving
in competitive self-congratulatory
ecstasy, how my fifth grade teacher
kept blinking at the grainy black-and-white
TV we all crowded around as if trying to
wash what she saw from her mind.
The playoffs: My son holds his trophy aloft.
He scans the crowd. I refuse to catch his eye.
His gaze never aligns with my field of vision.

Halloween Pattern

What type of mermaid do you want to be?
Is there more than one kind?
Do you mean like Ariel?
No, like Poseidon.
Isn't he more of a merman?
    Shoulder shrug.
I need a trident and a crown.
Do you want a tail?
Yes, with sparkly scales
glittered with stars
and fork tines
gilded and sharp.
The invitation says:
No weapons of any kind.
I need it for protection.
Protection from whom?
Cowboys and Indians.
In the sea? *At the party.*

Nocturne

They call it the noonday demon
as if it escapes its midnight shackles
to squat on your chest, eclipse
all passion, and lay flaccid as a tongue
dipped in volcanic ash. My son faces
an old-fashioned bogeyman who sulks
and sighs in his upside-down cage,
waiting for a bedside tremor to unbolt
his lock. When cortisol pools
in the stomach, it acts like a virus.
No: it is a nighttime circus
of shadow trainers conducting imps
on his Thomas the Tank Engine rug.
Awaiting dawn's whistle, my son
puts his faith in the single turquoise
impaled on the web of the dream-
catcher I hang from his doorknob.
The Navajo, I tell him, had it right.

The Robbery

Not six miles out of Cold Springs,
we were beset by highwaymen.
Four horses, a milky white, a calico,
a black, and a brown, surrounded us.

I know horseflesh and these steeds
were under duress. Their riders
twitched in bespoke tanned saddles
as I pitched a low whistle. Everyone

knows a calico has a sweet tooth.
We had a foal who liked his hay
flavored with ginger, trained to hunt
and prance to my father's harmonica.

They seized all, save for some gold
coins sewn into my petticoats.
With the knife at my son's throat,
I kept still my undergarments' jingle.

A Liberal Is a Rare Vintage

for Dianthe Lusk (1801-1832)

Feeding an army is nothing like catering for the Big House.
First, starch the stomach, sparing the meat and salt.
Add herbs for fragrance and digestion. A big pot and
a wood-fire are essential. Heat being the most needful thing.

John Brown's beloved first wife learned to bake his bread
with superfine, stone-milled flour that ascended an airy crumb.

On this floating tartine, he wanted only plum preserves stewed
in their own syrup. He shared with his soldiers, who slathered
their bread, greedily sucking the black glue from their fingers,
until they ran bowlegged into the grove to relieve their bowels.

These small black bulbs grew in heavy tumorous clusters
and ripened slowly until the last day of August.
I plucked plums as if they were wine grapes for a giant
then simmered them with their skins into a smoky tar.

He tipped his hat and paid for the jar in script we saved
then burned to keep warm our first Michigan winter.

The Garden of the West

This signature dish honors the Jubilee Singers'
performance in Paw Paw at Sinai Presbyterian.
Malinda found a notice stamped with a woodcut
of a woman who resembled Mary—her face a heart,
dark lashes sweeping the round peaks of her cheeks,
mouth an open oval of praise—in her son's satchel.

They paid the twenty-five cents offering to ensure a seat.
The choir ushered in like a storm front in black robes.
Mary stepped into the light. A small girl with a voice that
swelled from her shoulders into a muscular, melodious alto
recalling the toil of the field, the sufferings of the way station,
the burrowing and winnowing of freedom's crossing.

He brought her a flaming bowl, his face as red as the garnish,
which the singer politely refused, pointing first to her throat
then to the pool of bourbon left by the last extinguished flicker.

Arrival

My boy walks a curvature of raked
sand, windswept and rosy.
Above the ruins, watchful cannons
point eastbound and down.

The landscape could be that of a Saturnal moon.
Volcanic sculptures rise
from an aquamarine pool as a school of parrotfish
meander, unbelievably cobalt.
It's like another planet, he says, but for the glass,
green and silk-shattered,
so that one has to leap from rock to shore.

The Turtle Cure

Found, floating in the Great Pacific Garbage Patch,
on a scroll of parchment curled in a bottle of sea glass,
the following:

> Take the pistle of a green turtle, which lives in the sea, dry it with
> a moderate heat, pound it in a mortar to powder, and take of this
> as much as will lye upon a shilling, in beer or the like, ale or white
> wine, and in a very short time it will do the cure.

Of all Malinda's recipes, this is the one that wounds.
First, seduce a green turtle. This will require an adept manipulation
of scent and sound. Do not introduce terror: it will corrupt the meat.
Jasmine flowers crushed in bourbon is a soothing lure. Alternatively,
stalk the swamp with a crossbow. The terroir will be thick with nutria.
Do not be tempted to substitute, simmering will not silken their flesh.
A spear fisher can free dive 100 feet with one breath, which she will expel
before loosing her harpoon.

When I spoon the peat-brown broth into my mouth, it burns a sore tucked
deep in my left gum, an instant allergen that recalls an outing with my parents,
dressed in Sunday best to breakfast at Brennan's—after the Vieux Carré is
drowned by rising waters, loggerheads will reclaim the culinary institution's tablecloths
and toast twinkling glasses of claret with hawksbills—where I had a similar reaction
to their famed first course: turtle soup with sherry and hot pepper sauce.

Uncanny, the resemblance between the original, which appears on page six
under "to impress" and the proven remedy for kidney stones all the rage
in the seventeenth century, which is to say, from Barbados to Liverpool,
no turtle went uncastrated.

Mr. Coconut

A shipwreck survivor
would be glad to discover this lifeline
hairy, instead of honeydew, recumbent leftover
of a longtail's picnic. My son, who has never known thirst or
scurvy, befriends, photographs, takes it into his bed, and names it.
He suffers from canine hunger; a coconut will serve.
Gently, I explain, it will not clear customs.
Why not break it open?

I hope for sorbet, that piña colada
will emerge, and I can spoon out its creamy flesh.
We have no knife, and so recruit a chiseled rock.
The coconut easily defeats limestone
but I persist even as he howls in protest,
then turns gleeful as it refuses to crack.

Don't drink it, a fisherman warns
as we march towards the beach,
the water will be brackish,
a vinegary, jellyfish stew.
We succeed in piercing the outer shell,
its furry overcoat,
before we concede,
returning it to the Gulf Stream
to bewitch the next generation of explorers.

What Makes the Dutch Antilles

In water as blue, I found this pearl
cradled in a conch's intestines like its last egg.
When I drill a hole for a chain, it collapses;
the flesh, however, is more resilient, it gives
only when doused with pepper and lime. Lyme,
a mercurial substance, can be drizzled over a mass
grave and still a grove of almond trees will rise,
slender and middle-aged, from fresh mulch;
their branches press peach blossoms into the canopy
Van Gogh paints in honor of his nephew's birth,
a shade more azure than ethereal, like an upside-down sea.
So maybe I'm really falling instead of floating, sleeping
instead of sipping my mojito at a lime-in, catching
the sharp acid of citrus muddled by mint and regret.

Interview with a Zombí

Zora Neale finds a sugar cube in her valise.
This one has a sweet tooth, and molasses
is known to loosen tongues. Her Kréyol
is passable, but not as perfected as her French.
She has with her a portable lathe. Nothing fancy,
but to the deceased's family, it's a marvel.
A child in the corner, cashew-eyed, swollen-bellied,
snatches the white square as she extends her hand.
Replayed, the machine has captured an hour of drums.
Danse macabre, her lover whispers as they spoon.
Only a houngan would recognize its otherworldly rhythms.
A flicker illumines the shadowed railing of her balcony.
No, it's only fireflies, a trick, like the sugar's dulcet venom.
Everyone but her knows it's salt that's salvation.

Liberian Ballad

after Augustus Washington's *View of Monrovia from the Anchorage* (1856)

When Malinda met Mr. Vaughan on a night out in Greenville
you would have thought the talk would have been of faith
or livelihood. A nineteenth-century bachelor needed both
to gain a wife. A certain steadfast Temperance.

Instead he spoke of a grand voyage and proffered a pamphlet
engraved with a stoic crowd attentive to a preacher reading
from a Bible in a jungle. Will there be mountains? she asked,
accustomed to the elevated air zipping through the pines

enclosing the valley at the foot of the Great Smoky ridge
where she learned the names of edible wildflowers:
which to candy, the best pansies to petal a blush wedding
cake, the lavender to lavish. Persuaded by his proposal,

she carried violets instead of orange blossoms. Sapphires
studded Mr. Vaughan's waistcoat. He boasted gemstones
pebbled the bottomland, omitting that the colony lost
one in five to fever caused—it was believed—by bad

humours emitted from the swamp, which in fear they cleared
along with the eldest trees. In Washington's lithograph,
Monrovia is a port city on a hill indistinguishable from
San Francisco, a frontier they could pioneer as new pilgrims

plotting a feast at a round table where everyone was native.
He pointed to the dwarven shrubbery fencing the houses.
Each promised a garden. Would we find new names
in Liberia, she wondered, carved on the undersides of cairns

stacked on shores of embarkation? No, he said, the missionaries
want us to keep our Christian monikers, because Liberia will be
a Christian nation, populated by Christians like Mr. Vaughan,
who succumbed swiftly to a common malady, having lingered too
long in a stranger's land. Though entitled, she would never use his name.

A Curiosity

after *Mandingo* (1975)

I share a *Cure for Rheumatism,* a disease that ticks
in our bones, with my mother; it's a more benign
treatment than what appears in a plantation porn
scene on the veranda of the Big House in which
a charlatan places an enslaved toddler as footstool
for a master suffering from "the rheumatiz."
His yellowing toes curl on the boy's distended belly
as the "doctor" diagnoses. Why not try *sarsaparilla,*
prickly ash, cherry bark, bittersweet, and wintergreen boiled
each to a gallon with a quart of rum, three times daily?

███ Head Soup

Dress the head and boil ████   *remove* █ *bones* ████████
take all the meat ██████████████   *and chop fine* ████
██

sweet Margery ████████   *Stir* ████████████████
together ███████████████████████   *Make a hash*
             of the meat from the under jaw.
             Take the brains from the head.
beat ████████████████████████████   *after seasoning*
████████   *melt* ███████████████████████
   slowly.
Skin and slice the tongue ████████████████████████████████
             Stew dry.

[To Make] Magic

Oil
Laudanum
Chloroform
Sassafras
Hemlock
Cayenne
Cedar
Camphor
Alcohol

Split & Sew

We sent the boy Simon for the Negro doctress
with my sugar snaps wrapped in good linen.
She lived up Chuckey Mountain. In the spring
white trillium light the lime-lined path to her cabin.

A stone's throw from Shakerag Hollow, the
neighbors still didn't trouble her. More often than
not, she carried one of their brown bottles on rounds,
dispensing as needed for antiseptic or anesthesia.

She wrapped the first in a flour sack, I never held him.
The second she caught in a sweetgrass basket,
saved then buried the afterbirth. This one, she said,
you will keep, as she stitched me up, but no more.

She left a bouquet of tansy, rue, and pennyroyal
with instructions for brewing a tisane. This
secret pharmacopeia appears in my appendix,
disguised as *Elixir Paregoric*, decipherable
only to those who can read an *Evening Star* quilt.

Open Curtains

If it is barely spring,
orange tulips frame
my neighbors' bungalow—
a roguish backdrop
for the boys' white sneakers,
black & yellow hoodies.
They are up to nothing
or something.
I am listening
to their buzzing
but not hearing.
I am thinking
of my boy
on a parallel street
in a like formation
not regarded by me.
I read the same page
over & over until
when I look up,
they are gone.
The bruised shadows
of tulips loiter
in their wake.

Apologia

Today in the mail I received a handwritten
note from a person whose illegible signature
required that I google the address to discover
its provenance. Let me restate: its provenance
was benevolent privilege. So accustomed am I
to the casual pokes and missteps of daily
interaction that I failed to be offended by,
or maybe misremembered, the incident
obligingly related inside the card, imprinted
with an abstract collage of what I think was
an Asian carp, an invasive species my son
likes to fish for in the lake and let suffocate on
shore. He lures them with sweet corn. A kindness,
he says, because these carp have no restraint.
They obliterate biodiversity and we do not
want a lake that only holds one type of fish.

Tether

I could be underwater.
What's inside is out,
the air irradiated.
My legs draw up the silk.
I am a human pendulum,
but it's the globe that's spinning
comet dust everywhere.
Letting go seems improbable
but gravity turns out not to be
a permanent state of affairs, and I do.
Left to swing amidst aged oaks
spreading rumors of other
aerialists: there was the young lad
who did a deadly jig and the aged
midwife who hung so lightly and long.
I loose my hair, and it tickles their roots
while their arms shed spirals of helicopters,
empire's confetti, as I reach for the knot,
slip the yoke as easy as a newborn
spools into cottonwood ash.

Cooking in the Key of Nina

When I am struggling with one of Malinda's receipts,
or my son has had a fit, I put on "I Shall Be Released."
Nina sings her intentions, and my heart chakra
unwinds like the tattoo of a coral heart embraced by
thorns—what my son will emblazon on his tricep
just before mounting a cobalt Harley on his sixteenth
birthday. If Simone can't help you find an easement,
laudanum will do the trick. If Malinda was such a good
cook, she should have included a recipe for freedom
pie: one bite to teleport all kinfolk North.

Chaney

I packed the dishes in saddlebags between copies of *The North Star*,
what issues we had not passed clandestinely on to other subscribers.
All items in the pastry shop were sold or returned to lenders, save
these blue-and-white cups and saucers in which I served custard or tea.
A gift from my mother's mistress whose mother brought them from her
birthplace; a dowry from Delft. She named my mother Delf-ine to
remind her of that town and the subtropical island she fled to after
being widowed by a hurricane of all but her human property.
Their mismatched sturdiness lent an elegance, a charm that led ladies
to linger over their little cakes. When we unpack in Michigan, all the cups
have chipped, all the saucers have fissures, but I use them anyway.
A reminder of what cannot be broken.

Fiddle (A Duo)

Aspirate a note, a sounding in a silo
entombed beneath wet sand where
indigo, salt, sugar, tobacco, cotton, rice
preserve a desperate hybrid crop.

Mouth organ at midnight.
One woman supine, another
quadrilles—all blush crinoline
and caramelized curls—in a swamp:
what slithers and steams, moss.

Antiseptic sun, bleached-bone
sheets twist in the first stirrings
of a storm held offshore by
a single, vibrating chord
as the laundress digs for clams
in the shoal, starlit and moon-dark.

The string snaps. A rupture.

II.

Black infants in America are now more than twice as likely to die as white infants — 11.3 per 1,000 black babies, compared with 4.9 per 1,000 white babies, according to the most recent government data — a racial disparity that is actually wider than in 1850, 15 years before the end of slavery, when most black women were considered chattel.

Linda Villarosa, *The New York Times Magazine*

And hardly had she left her bed and been able to walk again without pain, hardly had the children returned home from the homes of the neighbors, when she began to have her fifth child.

Nella Larsen, *Quicksand*

Outcome

Her serve is 125 miles an hour
but she cannot outrun this.

She has won, has published,
but she cannot outwrite this.

She has starred, has danced,
but she cannot out-twirl this.

She has flown, sung, and swam,
released from parallel bars,
stuck a vault without stutter
but always the eclipse awaits.

Anomaly: when a thing happens that
the accumulated data cannot validate.

You tell yourself: this is not life-threatening.
You tell yourself: you can afford to raise or bluff.
You tell yourself: you can enunciate yourselves out.

The Talented Tenth assembles a league of doulas.
They edge the black of their capes with starlight.

None of this helps. None of this will save you.

Linea Negra

How your shoes have helped me track time.
That summer on the vineyard your feet grew
taller than your shoulders. We went through
two pairs of tourist-trap sandals priced for a full-
grown man. The doctor traces your growth curve
illustrating how the base expands to support
the scaffolding. The bones with their industrious
ambitions stretch the inter-tissue over a golden
foundation. The sun has already left its mark.
I want to be your warden, but you inch closer
to its light, making it impossible to keep you
in view as you turn the corner, enter the school,
flee the courthouse, eschew the hospital, escape—
I pray and pray—the grave.

Diastasis Recti

Always she heats the water, sharpens the blade.
She hopes to use one, never the other.

The midwife sets her mind wholly on heavenly things
and makes ready to catch.

In a quotidian birth, a retinue of childless girls
assist in preparation of their own lying-ins.

This death will make the holiest sonnet: its pathos
evidenced by its excess, its hushed anticipation.

The way the last fruit to fall from an
overburdened tree is unwanted, uneaten

except by rot and its court of flies, maggots, and the
occasional squirrel who excretes its seed in virgin soil.

Home Birth Suite

What if we have the baby at home? (laughter)
Did I ever tell you about a placental abruption?
You don't want to clean up that much blood.

Think 1970s: Jaws, Carrie, The Shining*'s elevator.*
What is your marital status? I already told you.
I don't have insurance. A home birth is cheaper.

You are high-risk. I'm only ____ years old. (All of you are high-risk.)
Just breathing. Just drinking coffee.
A doula? Save your money for college tuition.

We have a new birthing center; you won't [want to] leave.
But on the tour, we lingered in the operating room.
That's where you'll have your C-section.

I want a natural birth. *What is natural?*
Do you feel safe at home? I already answered.
Are you married? I already answered.

The husband will always choose the wife. (Is this your husband?)
[don't] Let them cut me. *You can try again.*
I will never do this again.

Ophidiophobia

At the end of this poem, our couple will have
suffered their first loss. Three shadows held hands
until they reached the summit and it struck.
In the days before cell phones, they lingered
at the trailhead, consulted the map, refilled
two water bottles, and unleashed Hendrix.
He bounded ahead, pausing to nuzzle a golden-
doodle that lifted its chin in disdain. The woman
smiled falsely at its owner and stared, somewhat
wistfully, at her inflated abdomen. Barely dawn,
they were still watchful for mountain lions,
known to return late from a night outside the den.
In reward for their vigilance, they glimpsed a blur
of fur that paused, and lasered hazel-eyed hunger
from its glance, before it recalled it disliked the taste
of humans and was camouflaged by beige rock-face.
Hendrix's black coat stunned white. If only they'd
known how to gather Cesar's cure for snakebite:
a concoction of wild horehound and plantain.
The remedy's proven potency freed its inventor,
but prolonged, for its afflicted recipients, clearing
Carolina swamps and floating rice, that life.
Only after the whimper did they hear the rattle,
the snickering slide into the underbrush.
By the time the sun was high, their dog was gone.
Later, they will tell themselves it was preparation.

Strawberry Creek

On the milk path to the boarded well,
        our sons find rusted hooks and lures
scattered by the woodpile.

Prospectors, nuggets for eyes, iron for blood,
        sifted sediment until one settled
the floodplain, built a cabin that has stood empty

for a century until: we unfurl sleeping bags, unload
        while our children make for the crick.
At seven, I walked its meandering mile

without wetting a toe in its foam. Now, browning
        mountains accent desiccated clusters
of berries that once ripened along its banks.

A new sign renames the waterway after the wild
        accessory fruit that still dwindles
in moss-topped granite beds. Bucolic moniker,

its utterance a hunger for early summer,
        appears on each village storefront,
jar label, and gas pump. We exchange

pleasantries in the ice cream parlor.
        With practiced ease, the scooper lets
by dead nigger creek slip off her tongue.

Now, watery chatter triggers my insomnia
        but does not lather the traces
of the lone black prospector's plea.

How to Avert a Duel in the Hotel Lounge

In our marriage's infancy of paper and metal,
I learned you are slow to anger. I can push far
beyond most men's tolerance and be forgiven,
yet you can hold a grudge against a toddler,
whose rejection will never let you go. So
when an acquaintance touches my shoulder
and a curtain drops like a guillotine over
your eyes, I taste blood in my mouth—
the metallic bite makes me glance at my glass
of Cabernet, its viscosity impenetrable in the
bar's backlight. In his impertinent wake, the type
of woman who turns heads—hers is shaved,
a bronze globe embedded with eyes of shattered
sea glass—steps between us, cinching our square
tight with her perfume: crushed dogwood petals
with a base note of rot. By turns, the press
of bodies astonishes the mixologists. How
unquenchable the thirst of writers. How
it is rumored the last conference shuttered
the bar once the last whiskey was poured.
With a half-embrace, she reaches around,
retrieves her scotch and soda, and swallows it
so fast my stomach cramps. Distracted, I miss
the green bottle in your fist. Moments later,
a dark spill glazes his forehead like ganache.
The two of them repel apart. This violence
that holds our vows fitfully together.

Mocktails on Mars

I'm thinner in denim than I've ever been.
I'm Zoë Kravitz, and my boyfriend is a hipster

with a mixed sidekick who waits at the bar
while we float upstairs to search for a table.

We secure a booth on the ceiling that encircles
a smoky quartz chandelier, its shimmering: pears

of anticipation. Before our party arrives,
I straddle him upside-down on maroon velvet.

His mouth is leather and metal. Parliament,
my miniskirt—all the easement we need.

The sidekick straps in our guests. A waiter ascends
with a menu. He pulls out. Semen clots in zero gravity.

I order a lilac foam, neat. How I've lived so long
in enemy territory; my inner galaxy integrated.

My Name Ain't Scarlett, It's Butterfly

I have to squat like a pro-wrestler
to coax a single pound from my ass,
and so, despite last night's hard rain:
no excuses, BlackGirlsRun.
Like the patterollers are after our tails.
Like this unleashed puppy pawprints
my size nine Lululemon with crotch-control
and fluorescent stitching so I can be seen
clearly through the spatter of mud season.
This is not a nourishing volcanic mask.
This is earthworm element,
quick to swallow trail-runners
to the shin before the first blaze.
Instead of water, I carry a nightstick.
Tell myself the hooded man
that steps out of the copse
before the first swinging bridge,
the one with bluebells framing
the other side, is not a troll.
Pray its spine will bear my weight.

Mama Said Knock You Out

after Nathaniel Mary Quinn's *This is Life*

I am always on the lookout
for beauty in the quotidian.
Each slice of paper marks
a suture in time. Minutes
might be bullets, and I'm
rocking a glass cradle.
What harm did I do you
on my knees is what Milk-
man's mother prayed in
Song of Solomon. He didn't
defend her name. Just took.
His sisters, artificial florists,
snipped petals of hot pink
taffeta, like those adorning
Miss Chairs and Mister *Charles*,
but not *Big Bertha*. She's alright
as she is: lacquered lips, raspberry
pillbox, pinstripes at the ready.

Red Truck

Watching for what might come
out of the woods instead of the road,
I miss the engine's quiet stall.
A hawk dives towards the tree line.
The deafening music of the plateau
is a dissonant composition of bees
gorging on white clover, wrestling
minks, and catcalling chickadees.
The opening bars of "Free Bird"
perforate my solace—its intrusion
a soundtrack to a hate crime.

Dixie Moonlight

A flood, like Noah's flood,
like after Katrina, like the
Mississippi's goddamn muddy
Blues, like Sylvia on death,
or Toni on slavery, like swag
surfing over the breakwater,
the levees levitating,
water seeping up through
cracked foundations, like molasses,
drowning cows in a pasture
of sweet. This placental blood
is an abrupt surprise.

Perfect Matte

The unnamed African woman who took a halting step off a ship
onto swampland in a Louisiana port had certain je ne sais quoi.
Call it survivor's sparkle. A corona that attracted the highest bids
in Congo Square and sent her straight to da big house. Beyoncé,
you and I wear the same shade of foundation: a tube of red
minerals culled from Yoruba, Seminole, Irish, French, and Spanish
earth blended seamlessly into a creolized clan of American Negro.
We share this common ancestress, but while she can be ridden
in a golden flounce, I am too tired to twerk, to wield the flat iron
to swallow the lemonade to cleanse the vessel to host a goddess.

Kiss & Tell, or the First Black Bachelorette

She has the skin of a papaya—
a thin translucent brown fissured with lava.
See her—high angled—in Rapunzel's tower window.

A chorus of rats just freed from Hamlin bid:
let down your hair. She can't. The tracks raised welts.
Every swing of her braid smarts like the lashes

gluing her bedroom eyes wide. They wake her
at the witching hour to ask which one will
receive the rose but she can't tell them apart.

A producer arrives with scissors & speculum.
When she resists, a malicious sprite unfurls
a scroll notarized by her own menstrual thumbprint.

Here is when you say I do, he says,
Look at the shotgun, I mean, the camera.
You are the network's most beautifulest thing.

Oracle at Venice Beach, 1995

Seeking an ancestral cipher against the grim statistics
of racial math, we bypassed the palm reader seated
under the adjacent tent. I want to say that her dreadlocks,
studded with the cowries she would cast for us, brushed
the ground like a cape. She knew your baby brother
would turn vegan then baker, that I would travel
to a colder coast and be caught between two men:
one would take my virginity, the other would be
my ride-or-die, but only if I kept quiet and discerned
the one to love from the one to leave. There must have
been more mundane news: birth or death, money
& romance—the predictable tithes of life. I forgot until
you told me—we hadn't spoken for a year—that it
was aggressive and genetic; that she had warned you
of female trouble; to not wait if you wanted offspring.
Now in the undercommons between girlhood & matronage,
I absorb her patois, sense the cowries warming in my fist.
She refused our money. She was not wrong.
What else—remember—did she say?

Weathering

None of us in the prenatal clinic are the right age.
We are climbing or descending the bell curve.
The 18-to-35-year-olds are still at happy hour;
they spend their petty cash on pedicures.

Think of your shoelace, the genetic counselor
says, benignly. The plastic tip that keeps the cotton
from unraveling. That's the telomere. It protects
your legacy. In your people, it has come off,
peeled away like a chimney from an F4 twister
by a toxicity that seeps and creeps until your
womb is all black mold in need of remediation.

All you glean from this prognosis: please
strap yourself into the stirrups, an audience
of white coats anticipates. This science
is for saving lives that matter, not salvaging slaves.
A nurse secures the shackles as the surgeon
shifts your paper gown to expose one breast.
He whispers what Cassiopeia must have said
to sturdy Andromeda before leaving her for
the Kraken: be not afeard, after this last trial;
you will be magnified, astral, a consolation.

Red Tide

We wade into a channel sluggish with pink foam,
like a tube of tomato paste has been squeezed
into the simmering salt-bath surrounding the sandbar.
There is no ferry or ferryman to bribe for passage.
Stirred by offshore storms, the organic shedding leaves
behind a wake of death; wakes death; fish do not wake;
they float capsized until low tide maroons them on
the sandy mound where prenatal yoga was held yesterday.

Another wave of cramps rips through my abdomen.
This is not a normal flow: it's gravity, invisible, insistent.
My link with the moon has been broken
as if it is the fault of the lunar cycle. What lunacy
there is in that expression. As I wait for the Lyft
that will take us to triage, a crimson fringe haloes the moon.
Viewed from the rearview mirror, it is an orange marble.
Omen-obsessed, I ask the driver: do you see that
blood-on-the-moon, and she says no: that is Mars.

Apricots

as in the baby was the size of an apricot the week
you told me at your favorite restaurant that you
were miscarrying right now as I pressed my cheek
against your ear and wished you happy birthday

Estrella Negra

i. pigment

a dark pharmacology
of marrow and excrement
creates a brightness, the painter
claims, like the extraction
of sunshine from cucumbers
in brine, a pepperwood smoke,
like eggplant on the tongue
globular, when sizzled in
rendered pork and aged to
a funk more French than foul.

ii. skin

before we became less concerned for
arboreal souls, so many mammals
gave up their outerwear for vellum.
what is inscribed on flesh takes
on a permanence. sacred stains
that we interpret as portents of
what will come and pass over.
the artist traces her stretch marks
with a quill soaked in indigo,
tattooing a scroll that is also
a map to a sunken city
of red clay carved deep in
Eritrean earth, a dollhouse
for a giant's granddaughter
who drops primates in one by one
until they forget how to swing
from vine to tree, take up
residence in square caves, and
teach each other table manners.

iii. model

what else but batik for a mantle?
a black that is really the blue of
an underwater cavern, den of sea
serpents and whale sharks, in its
depths and valleys you can
make out the bruise and burn
of whip and brand. what crown
but Caridad's, gifted from a
runaway star. if a woman
puts her eyes on this portrait,
then dies in childbirth without
extreme unction, her reward
will be a seat on Virgin Galactic.

We Are Stardust Brought to Life

Ok Navigator.
I need more to eat than some
Of these heifers on this mother.
Especially if each night we gone
Have a Funkadelic dance off.
How many years is light-years?
I know your mama must be proud.
Are you related to the Memphis
deGrasses or the Chicken Tysons?
I could a sworn. Soylent isn't
A smoothie; grits, eggs, and
Sausage biscuits is breakfast.
Why did we choose the one thing
We couldn't live without instead
Of the one thing we needed most?
I don't feel right calling myself
A colonist—this isn't the *Mayflower*
Or the *Nina*—Butterflies is how
I describe what we will be when
We come out these Teflon cocoons.
Another is Angels. It's only fair we
Take turns cooking, but say,
Why is hotdish always gumbo?
These spacesuits are tight.
They make my ass look tight.
Who voted for this color?
It's radioactive. Nine months
Of morning sickness then, poof.
We take turns watching Baby Channel.
It's addictive.
How come mine never comes on?
I stare until the earth becomes
A speck of powdered blue.
I'd have remembered if I'd seen her.

Notes

p. 7 "Marble Cake" *A Domestic Cook Book: Containing a Careful Selection of Useful Receipts for the Kitchen* (1866), p. 8.

p. 8 In "Wild Yeast," "f'om de kitchen to de big woods" and "buried elbow-deep" from Paul Laurence Dunbar's "When Malindy Sings" and "Dinah Kneading Dough," respectively.

p. 9 "Restoring the Hair to Its Original Color" from *A Domestic Cook Book*, p. 38.

p. 12 "A Tempest in a Teapot." *A Domestic Cook Book*. p. 12.

p. 16 Sycorax is Caliban's mother in William Shakespeare's play *The Tempest*. She makes no appearance in the play.

p. 18 In 1986, the Space Shuttle *Challenger* exploded, killing all crew members on board, including a schoolteacher intending to conduct lessons from space.

p. 22 In 1859, the abolitionist John Brown led a raid on the arsenal at Harper's Ferry in the hopes of igniting a slave rebellion. Dianthe Lusk, his first wife, died in childbirth.

p. 25 The offset section is taken in part from Richard Ligon's *A True & Exact History of the Island of Barbados* (1657).

p. 30 "A Curiosity" *A Domestic Cook Book*, p. 38.

p. 31 "Head Soup" *A Domestic Cook Book*, p. 35.

p. 32 "[To Make] Magic" *A Domestic Cook Book*, p. 35.

p. 38 Chaney, a conjunction of china and money, is Virgin Island slang for the bits of Danish porcelain that wash up intermittently on the island. These remnants, which children use as currency and artists often repurpose, are a reminder of their colonial history.

p. 41 "Why America's Black Mothers and Babies Are in a Life-or-Death Crisis" By Linda Villarosa. *The New York Times Magazine.* April 11, 2018. Web. https://www.ny times.com/2018/04/11/magazine/black-mothers-babies-death-maternal-mortality .html.

p. 41 *Quicksand* by Nella Larsen. New York: Alfred A. Knopf, 1928.

p. 44 During pregnancy, a brown line bisecting the stomach due to hyperpigmentation, is known as the Linea Negra.

p. 45 Diastasis Recti is the postpartum separation of the abdominal muscles during pregnancy.

p. 47 Ophidiophobia is the fear of snakes.

p. 47 "The Negro Cesar's Cure for Poison" was published in *The South-Carolina Gazette*, May 14, 1750.

p. 51 Butterfly McQueen (1911-1995) played Prissy, the maid, of Scarlett O'Hara in *Gone With the Wind* (1939).

p. 52 Milkman is the nickname given to a character in Toni Morrison's *Song of Solomon* (1977) after he is seen nursing far beyond the time after which a child is typically weaned.

p. 61 The line "sunshine from cucumbers," is from colorist George Field in 1856, qtd from Simon Schama's article, "Treasures from the Color Archive." https://www .newyorker.com/magazine/2018/09/03/treasures-from-the-color-archive

Field wrote: "The world rubbed its eyes with astonishment and truly it seemed as wonderful to produce the colours of rainbow from a lump of coal, as to extract sunshine from cucumbers."

p. 63 The title "We Are Stardust Brought to Life" is taken from Neil deGrasse Tyson's *Astrophysics for People in a Hurry.* New York: W.W. Norton & Company, 2017, p. 17.

Acknowledgments

Grateful acknowledgment to the editors of the following journals who first published these poems:

"Outcome," "Tether," and "How to Avert a Duel in the Hotel Lounge" in *The Rumpus*.
"Apologia" and "Oracle at Venice Beach, 1995" in *The Journal*.
"The Turtle Cure" in *Blackbird*.
"Wild Yeast" and "Kiss & Tell, or the First Black Bachelorette" in *Plume*.

Thanks to the University of Michigan William L. Clements Library for the facsimile of *A Domestic Cook Book: Containing a Careful Selection of Useful Receipts for the Kitchen* by Mrs. Malinda Russell, An Experienced Cook. Paw Paw, Michigan, 1966.

This book would not have been produced without the support of the Emily Mead Baldwin Award and the UW Division of the Arts. My everlasting gratitude to Christine Stroud and Autumn House Press. Thanks to the Sewanee Writers' Conference for the Walter E. Dakin Poetry Fellowship, during which I wrote several of these poems, hiked, and made the acquaintance of Charlotte Pence, my "fellow" fellow, a tremendous poet and gracious reader. I lift up Janean Dilworth-Bart, as well as the doulas and healthcare workers of Harambee Village for your efforts to increase the birth outcomes for women of color. I deeply appreciate the support of family and friends, especially my sister-moms in J & J, former and current Mochas, for linking arms around our children. Finally, and always, thanks to Amaud: my first, my last, my everything.

New and Forthcoming Releases

under the aegis of a winged mind by makalani bandele ♦ Winner of the 2019 Autumn House Poetry Prize, selected by Cornelius Eady

Circle / Square by T. J. McLemore ♦ Winner of the 2019 Autumn House Chapbook Prize, selected by Gerry LaFemina

Hallelujah Station and Other Stories by M. Randal O'Wain

Grimoire by Cherene Sherrard

Further News of Defeat: Stories by Michael X. Wang ♦ Winner of the 2019 Autumn House Fiction Prize, selected by Aimee Bender

Skull Cathedral: A Vestigial Anatomy by Melissa Wiley ♦ Winner of the 2019 Autumn House Nonfiction Prize, selected by Paul Lisicky

No One Leaves the World Unhurt by John Foy ♦ Winner of the 2020 Donald Justice Prize, selected by J. Allyn Rosser

In the Antarctic Circle by Dennis James Sweeney ♦ Winner of the 2020 Autumn House Rising Writer Prize, selected by Yona Harvey

Creep Love by Michael Walsh

The Dream Women Called by Lori Wilson

For our full catalog please visit: http://www.autumnhouse.org